Poemas de la Isla

Poemas de la Isla

poems by
Josefina de la Torre

translations by
Carlos Reyes

EWU
P·R·E·S·S

EASTERN WASHINGTON UNIVERSITY PRESS

SPOKANE, WASHINGTON 2000

ACKNOWLEDGMENTS

Gracias mil a las siguientes personas, sin las cuales hubiera sido imposible llevar a cabo este libro de traducciones:/ Many thanks to the following people, without whom bringing this book of translations to completion would have been impossible: Simone Alin, Elizabeth Atly, Christopher Howell, Selena Millares, María Presentación Sánchez-Cascado, Greg Simon, Steven White. . . . Y un fuerte abrazo a mi socio y buen amigo Greg Simon por su apoyo y ayuda.

Un agradecimiento muy especial a / A very special thank-you to: Morten Vilhelm Keller y Martha Velásquez Keller de la Fundación Valparaíso en Mojácar (España).

Además, reservo algunas palabras particulares de agadecimiento para la profesora Selena Millares por todo lo que ha hecho por mi y para mi en este esfuerzo.

Y por supuesto dedico este libro con mucha admiración y mucho respecto a su autora: Josefina de la Torre Millares.

Cover and Book Design by Scott Poole

Eastern Washington University Press is grateful for a grant from *The Program for Cultural Cooperation between Spain's Minister of Culture and United States Universities* which helped to support publication of this volume.

Library of Congress Cataloging-in-Publication Data

Torre, Josefina de la.
[Poemas de la Isla. English & Spanish]
Poemas de la Isla. poems / by Josefina de la Torre; translation by Carlos Reyes
    p. cm.
ISBN 0-910055-59-9 (cloth alk. paper) -- ISBN 0-910055-58-0 (pbk. alk. paper)
    1. Reyes, Carlos, 1935- II. Title.

PQ6670.O663 P6413 2000
861'.64--dc21   99-059814

Contents

Translator's Note

Originally this volume *Poemas de la isla* was to have contained only the original *Versos y estampas* (1927) in its entirety, with selections from *Poemas de la isla* (1930). Since meeting Josefina and discovering more of her work, it seems fitting to me to augment the book with some work never published before in book form, as well as a more recent poem. Therefore, I have included both "Puerto de Mar" ("Sea Port"), for which Josefina wrote both words and music, and "Allí, junto a la cama" ("There, by the Bed"), from *Medida del tiempo (Time's Measure)* written after the death of her second husband Ramon Corroto (d. 1980).

For those who are interested in the women poets of the Generation of 1927 and want to read more about them and Josefina de la Torre, I suggest a lengthy article replete with photographs "Mujeres del 27" (Insula No. 557, Mayo, 1993), and the recently published *Antologia de poetisas del 27* (Madrid, Editorial Castalia, 1999), which contains in addition to its four hundred pages of poetry over one hundred pages of introduction, notes and bibliography.

Introduction

Josefina de la Torre during the heyday of the Generation of '27.

The language of the soul is memory.

—*Luis Rosales*

It is Cervantes Day in Madrid, April 23, 1999. I am sitting in an apartment on the banks of the Manzanares River, listening to 92-year-old Canary Island poet Josefina de la Torre tell me about the day she and Pedro Salinas sat on the grass, reading their poems to each other . . .

I had been searching without success for Josefina de la Torre—as time and circumstances permitted—since 1987 when I translated the selection of her poems found in Gerardo Diego's prestigious *Poesía española contemporánea* (1934). I knew, or thought I knew, she had been born in 1907, but mystery surrounded this member of the famed "Generation of 1927." Was she still alive, and if so, where was she living? Despite her being published in anthologies of women poets through the years since 1934 (such as *Cien años de poesía femenina e hispanoamericana 1840-1940* [1943] and *Poesía femenina española viviente* [1954]), as well as *Marzo incompleto* which first appeared in the periodical *Fantasía*,) few people in literary circles seemed to have heard much of her recently, and none knew of her exact whereabouts. Curiously, even the *Dictionary of the Literature of the Iberian Peninsula* (1993)—a work I have only recently discovered—is ambivalent about when she was born, and notes that she *probably* died in the 1970s, although the editors said they could not confirm her death.

In 1989, Christopher Howell struck gold when he discovered in the University of Kansas Library, de la Torre's *Poemas de la isla*, edited by poet and critic Lázaro Santana and published that same year in the Canary Islands. The book collected the original *Versos y estampas* (1927), *Poemas de la isla* (1930), *Marzo incompleto* (1968) and the previously unpublished *Medida del tiempo*. In addition to providing me with a larger segment of her work for translation, Santana's introduction, which incorporated biographical notes from *Poesía española contemporánea*, also gave me a bit more material about the poet's life until the 1980s and included work written early in that decade. But even his suggestion that she might be writing at the time the book was published could not, of course tell me if Josefina de la Torre was still alive in 1999 and if she was in the Canary Islands, Madrid or anywhere in Spain at all.

Finally, an American friend and Lorca translator, Steven F. White, who had heard of my translation project and was teaching and living in Madrid, scratched around and began to get results. After a dozen or so telephone calls, he contacted Selena Millares, a Madrid University literary professor and critic from the Canary Islands, and a distant relative of de la Torre herself. Millares had discovered that the poet was alive, well and living in Madrid. She had also come up with her address and telephone number. At the urging of Steve White and my wife, Elizabeth Atly, I decided to go and meet the poet whose book I had just finished translating and whose work had fascinated me for more than a decade.

Selena Millares telephoned Josefina, held a preliminary meeting with her, and arranged a day when I would go to her house, meet her, interview her on video, and look through her papers. Our plans took on some urgency when Steve White read in *El País* that Josefina's contemporary Ernestina de Champourcín, also one of the few surviving members of the Generation of 1927, had died on March 30, 1999 at the age of 93. Josefina and Ernestina were the only women represented in 673 pages of Gerardo Diego's *Poesía española contemporánea*!

Shortly before my arrival in Madrid, Steve White found an antiquarian book dealer who claimed to have a book called *Poemas canarios* by Josefina de la Torre. I was intrigued at the possibility of getting my hands on it, but I knew of no book with that title by de la Torre, so I was very curious. I suspected and hoped it would be a first edition of *Poemas de la isla*.

Steve and I took the Metro to the Puerta del Sol and went down the side streets looking for the Filobiblión. We stopped only long enough for me to withdraw thousands of pesetas from a money machine. Steve had warned me the book would not be cheap, and there would be no bargaining, since it was one of a kind.

By the time we arrived at the shop, I was ready to buy the book, whatever the cost. Steve had made a good case. How could I be her translator, he asked, and not own even one of her books? And wouldn't it be impressive if I showed up to meet her and asked her to sign a first edition of the book for me?

It was indeed *Poemas de la isla* . . . And the price? Seven pesetas, it said on the back cover. But that was 1930, when the book was first published . . . I leave it to the reader's imagination what that little first edition cost me in April, 1999!

I must say that the days leading up to my interview were most nerve-wracking. I began to realize the dangerous presumption that lurked in translating someone else's poetry. As translators we assume the authors of the original works are eager to have their works translated into another language, thereby extending their readership and reputation. But are they as enthusiastic as we? I had only recently begun translating living poets and had never actually met one of them face to face. How would Josefina feel about the translation? I had extensively translated her work without her permission. How would she feel about that? How did Josefina feel about translations in general? The whole trip had come together so quickly I hadn't really had time to consider these matters fully.

I had been assured by everyone involved that Josefina was impressed and grateful that someone from so far away was coming to rediscover her and publish her work, and thus help in a small way to bring her out of obscurity and back into her rightful place in contemporary Spanish poetry. But to the male dominated literary establishment in Madrid it must have been uncomfortable and somewhat embarrassing to have an outsider point out to them what they had essentially ignored and forgotten since 1934—this important surviving poet of the Generation of 1927 who felt "pushed out, buried in ashes, erased by forgetfulness," to quote from one of her later poems ("Mis amigos de entonces" from *Medida del tiempo)*.

Our meeting was set for 5:30 p.m., Friday, the 23rd of April. Selena Millares met with Steve and me at the Café del Real on the Puerta del Sol. We had coffee and chatted. From that point on, anxiety began to leave me. We took a cab to Josefina's apartment and arrived promptly at 5:30. We were welcomed graciously by Josefina and her friend and "secretary" Maríapresen (Maria Presentación Sánchez-Cascado). Maríapresen was extremely helpful during our visit, always ready with an explanation or detail. A journalist from the Canary Islands and a Madrid press photographer were already there. I presented Josefina with books I had brought as gifts. She signed documents from Eastern Washington University Press giving me permission to translate and publish her poems. I brought out the first edition copy of *Poemas de la isla* and asked her to inscribe it for me, which she did, smiling.

After many photographs were taken, I set up the video camera, then joined Josefina and Selena on the sofa where we began our conversation. I asked Josefina first about a poem that appears in *Medida del tiempo,* (Measure of Time). This poem, which bears an epigraph from Luis Rosales, "The language of the soul is memory," begins by listing all those legendary figures of literature from the Generation of 1927, whom Josefina knew personally.

> My friends of those days,
> those of you who read my verses
> and listened to my music:
> Luis, Jorge, Rafael,
> Manuel, Gustavo

> Enrique, Pedro, Juan,
> Emilio, Federico . . .

As I read her those verses, she filled in the last names. Luis . . . Buñuel, Jorge . . . Guillén, Rafael . . . Alberti, Manuel . . . Altolaguirre, Gustavo . . . Durán, Pedro . . . Salinas, Juan . . . Larrea, Emilio . . . Prados, Federico . . . García Lorca.

I asked her about Lorca, whom she had referred to as "The gypsy of the sweet smile, of burnt sugar" in an early poem ("Conocimiento de Federico García Lorca, el 28 de abril de 1927" / "Meeting Federico García Lorca the 28th of April, 1927.") Yes, she remembered him. He was charming and likeable, she said. The smile on her face and the light in her eyes said much more than the words.

Of all the names mentioned above, it was Pedro Salinas who probably influenced Josefina the most, as her reminiscences of him suggest. He wrote the wonderfully lyrical prologue to *Poemas de la isla* and—as critics such as Angel Valbuena Prat have pointed out—was the one who encouraged her to write "the light sea breeze of a poem" so characteristic of that book.

The poem from *Medida del tiempo* is a quiet complaint of one nurtured as a promising young poet, only to be left behind by her influential mentors, to wither and be neglected by the Spanish literary establishment for the next half century. That was the reason I wanted to ask her about the poem. I was particularly interested in the way the poem ended:

> And though it may happen
> that the winds of fate will bring us together again
> I don't know in which city that will be
> and if a day will come
> when I feel discovered again.

I asked her point blank if my coming to visit her in Spain had made her feel, on this day, in her apartment, rediscovered. Whether she misunderstood the question, or simply didn't hear it, I got no definite response. But when the journalist from the Canary Islands, Alicia Mederos, asked her a similar question, she certainly responded in the affirmative. Medero's question was: "What do you think of the initiative of this man who has come so far to meet you and publish your work?"

"I think it is wonderful," Josefina answered. What she inscribed in my copy of *Poemas de la isla* leaves no doubt: "To Carlos Reyes who has had the courage to come from so far away to find me and my poetry."

Josefina de la Torre wrote her first poem when she was seven years old. Though she no longer remembered what it was called, she did recall it was dedicated to Benito Pérez Galdós, Spain's most prolific novelist, and without a doubt the Canary Islands' most notable literary figure. Had she known him personally? No. But she did sing at a memorial gathering for him in 1920. She and Pérez Galdós were distant relatives.

Santana, in his introduction to *Poemas de la isla* (1989), describes Josefina as the ideal portrait of a woman of the vanguardia of the 1920s. (In addition to the details of her life mentioned earlier, she owned and drove her own car, in a time when women were not allowed to vote much less drive automobiles.) When I asked her if she considered herself a feminist or a woman ahead of her time, she answered with a modest *no*. Selena Millares asked if she preferred *la poeta* (the more modern and feminist term) to *poetisa*, poetess (the older and perhaps demeaning term). It made little difference to her, she said at first, then added she preferred *poetisa*.

Why were she and Ernestina de Champourcín the only women in Gerardo Diego's prestigious anthology *Poesía española contemporánea*? I knew the answer, but I wanted her to comment on why there were so few women represented among so many men. She said, "We weren't the only women in the Generation of 1927. There were others. Concha Méndez, for example."

"But you and Ernestina were the only two represented in Gerardo Diego's anthology," I insisted. "Why?"

"Because we were part of the group, he selected us. Because we were known." A modest answer perhaps, since Joaquín Artiles and Ignacio Quitana in *Historia de la literatura canaria* credit Josefina's inclusion to the success of her first books. Emilio Miró backs this up in his article "Poetisas del 27" (*Insula, 3, Mayo,*

1993) when he says that de la Torre's first book, *Versos y estampas* (1927), received high critical acclaim not only in Spain but in Latin America.

Miró goes on to say, however, that some have claimed the two women were included in the anthology for "gentlemanly reasons." (As a patronizing concession to the women?) Two women to represent contemporary Spanish poetry in the most prestigious anthology of the period? A book of 673 pages which contains twenty-five of the greatest male poets writing in Spanish—perhaps *of* all time— starting with Rubén Darío and including other greats such as Juan Ramón Jiménez, Antonio Machado, Federico García Lorca, Rafael Alberti, Luis Cernuda, Pedro Salinas.

In his introduction to the 1989 *Poemas de la isla*, Santana writes about events up to 1934, leaves without commentary the time up until 1943, then picks up the narrative again. Thus any information I have about those nine years comes from Josefina herself. "And the Civil War," I asked her? She said when the war started she couldn't return to the Canary Islands, so she stayed in Madrid. I asked her when she last made a trip to the Canaries. "About 30 years ago," she answered, to attend her brother Claudio's funeral. She told me she spent at least part of the Civil War in the Mexican Embassy in Madrid, where she sought political asylum. She was in the embassy long enough to become romantically involved with the ambassador's son, which for whatever reason caused a scandal in both families.

It goes without saying that in a civil war or any war there are those on both sides, and those who are caught in the middle. From the information I got during my conversation with Josefina, it seems likely that she, stranded in Madrid during the war, was one of the latter group.

After the war, Josefina began to write fiction. One example is *Memoria de una estrella*, a serialized "weekly novel" which tells the story of a starlet who becomes a housewife. It was written under the pseudonym of "Laura Comínguez," taken from a family name Comminges. She apparently enjoyed the writing of the weekly episodes and must have approached the writing in a playful way, as she often invited friends and family members to join her in the writing.

She was at the same time involved in acting. She played María von Trapp in a Spanish production of the musical about the Trapp family. In addition, Josefina had a major role in a long-running television series, *Anillos de oro* ("Golden Rings") until the early 1980s.

In those years of activity in other areas of the arts—when she was singing and acting—Josefina continued to write poetry. Her poetry from the 1940s to the 1960s is collected in *Marzo incompleto*, her third book, first published in the periodical *Fantasía*, but brought out in book form in 1968. She continued into the 1980s, writing the poetry which is found in her last book *Medida del tiempo*. Among her most recent poems are the tender elegies written after the death of her second husband, Ramón Corroto.

Josefina's apartment is a veritable museum of memorabilia. Along with pictures of her family, including a very charming one of her and Ramón Corroto, is one of Marlene Dietrich, affectionately inscribed to Josefina. Framed and hanging on the wall is a treasured handwritten poem to Josefina from Rafael Alberti, dated May 28, 1926. Selena took the poem down and read it to Josefina, who listened with quiet attentiveness and delight. Sadly, for whatever reason, if you search in Alberti's collected works, as I did, you will not find the poem "A Josefina de la Torre" published in the magazine *Verso y Prosa*. When Alberti's *Cal y canto* was published in 1927, the poem had become "Busca," with no mention of de la Torre.

Alberti died on October 28, 1999 at the age of 96, leaving Josefina as the last survivor of the Generation of 1927. Pointing out again how women poets were either ignored or neglected with regard to their role in Spanish poetry, newspapers stated that with his death the last member of the Generation was gone. With Josefina de la Torre still alive, it is not true, unless, as a woman, she is simply not considered a member.

Since Josefina was alive all those years between 1934 and 1999, and publishing, even if sporadically, why did she feel she was buried in the ashes of obscurity and why was she so hard to find? We can perhaps speculate on the reasons based on what we have discovered in brief biographical notes. Much of the reason lies with the Spanish Civil War. Her mentors and promoters during those years either were killed in the War (Lorca), or died (Salinas) or left Spain (Cernuda). With most of her mentors gone, she was no longer given the recognition and encouragement she received for her early work as a poet. Perhaps most of her creative energies were being spent on her acting instead of her writing, accounting for her diminished poetic output during the Civil War and years immediately following. During those years people may have known of her as an actress but not as a poet.

It should also be said that some of the other more high profile women, while in no sense undeserving, maintained their stature in part because they were associated with or married to famous male poets and publishers: Concha Méndez to Miguel Altolaguirre, Champourcín to Juan José Domenchina, to name two. Why were only two women, Ernestina de Champourcín and Josefina de la Torre, included in the most prestigious anthology of the 1930s, in an anthology dominated by male poets? The real answer, of course, may lie in the word *dominated*. The poetry scene in Spain has been, and to some extent still is dominated by male literary figures. That work by women poets such as María Figuera Ayamerich and Josefina de la Torre has not received fair critical acclaim is no secret. It is only recently that work has begun to emerge that accords to women their rightful place in the Generation of 1927. Articles like the one by Emilio Miró in *Insula* (No. 557, Mayo 1993) and the very recent *Antología de poetisas del 27*, published by Castalia in Madrid, with its ample selection of poetry and one hundred pages of notes and introduction also by Miró, go a long way in presenting the case for the significance and contribution of women poets to the Generation.

It is hardly surprising then—given the prevailing chauvinistic attitudes—that a book, *Poemas de la isla*, containing the life work of a significant woman poet, brought out in a limited edition in

1989 by a small governmental publishing house from the insular and provincial city of Las Palmas—far from the literary circles of Madrid—should be scarcely remarked on or reviewed. Nor should we be shocked to learn that ten years later a copy of the book, new or used, could not be found in any bookstore in that city. Isn't it ironic, and fortunate for us, that though the book barely made it to Madrid, a thousand miles from Gran Canaria, it found its way to Kansas.

We moved through history as we looked at Josefina de la Torre's autograph book filled with messages of good will from all the notables of her day as well as several wonderful pen and ink drawings.

From these and from existing photographs of Josefina, it is clear she was strikingly beautiful as a young woman. (She continues to be so in her maturity.) Santana has said, "She must have caused in her circle a fascinating impression, and not only for her talent; but also for her extraordinary beauty." Given that, it is not surprising that Josefina had numerous suitors, including poet Rafael Alberti, filmmaker Luis Buñuel—to whom she was "Muse," and well known actor Ramón Corroto, 26 years her junior, whom she married in 1977.

The afternoon was passing into evening. I thought perhaps we were taxing her strength with our presence and our questions. But she said brightly, "No, I am not tired, not one bit." So we continued our conversation.

I quoted to her the *ars poetica* she expressed in Gerardo Diego's 1934 anthology: "Poetry is tied to so much mystery, and because it is so unknown, I have never stopped to think what it is, I can only feel [what] it is."

When I asked her if after all those years she still felt the same about poetry, a definite *sí* was her reply.

How apropos is the quotation of Luis Rosales, "The language of the soul is memory." All the memories of Josefina de la Torre—

cinematic, theatrical, musical, literary, and especially poetic—are words of the soul. They come from this woman's lifelong involvement in the arts, this remarkable woman who embodied the femme avant garde of the 1920s, traveling in a world at that time generally reserved for men. So moved was I at dwelling briefly in that world of her memory, and spending time in the presence of this all-but-forgotten but still shining literary light of the Canary Islands, that as we left her apartment, I myself felt close to tears. Was it a day like this in April, seventy-two years ago, when she met Federico García Lorca? Or when she and Pedro Salinas sat out on the grass reading to each other? . . . Steve White, Selena Millares and I walked toward the metro station as the Madrid sun was setting on what for all of us had been an unforgettable, brilliant spring day.

—Carlos Reyes
Portland, Oregon
January 2000

PUERTO DE MAR

Viejo y sin luz,
eres febril
rincón de azar.
Todo el dolor
guardas en tí.
Ronco gemir,
noches sin paz.

Por tus tabernas al pasar
solloza el acordeón.
Las sombras cruzan y se van
huyendo de la canción.
Canción que el viento llevará
tan lejos que no ha de volver . . .
La muerte ronda sin cesar,
en el turbio amanecer.

De un viejo bar
al resplandor,
una mujer
se ve cruzar;
rota la voz,
fijo el mirar,
pronto el reír,
lento el andar.

Y por los muelles su canción
se lleva el rumor del mar.
El puerto duerme en derredor,
callado en la noche está.

SEA PORT

Ancient sea port
without light,
a feverish corner
of pure chance.
You keep all the pain
inside yourself.
Hoarse moan,
nights without peace.

The accordion sobs
from your taverns.
Shadows cross and depart,
fleeing from the song.
The wind will carry it
so far it may never return . . .
Death circles and circles
in the murky dawn.

From an ancient bar
a woman
is seen crossing;
in the brightness . . .
broken voice
fixed stare,
staccato laugh
languid walk.

Now along your docks song
carries the ocean's murmurs.
Everywhere the port is asleep,

Se escucha un grito en el confín . . .
¡La voz ya no responderá!
¡Oh, puerto viejo! ¿Qué hay en tí
que no te podré olvidar . . . ?

it's quiet through the night.
At the perimeter a cry is heard . . .
But now no voice will ever answer!
Oh! ancient port! What is it
that won't let me forget you?

ALLÍ, JUNTO A LA CAMA

Allí, junto a la cama,
están tus gafas.
Sus cristales vacíos
son como dos lagunas sin orillas.
Las cojo entre mis manos
y las contemplo absorta.
Detrás están tus ojos,
los presiento,
ahondando la mirada,
y las apoyo con ternura sobre el pecho,
como si tu cabeza reposara.
Las beso.
Son tus ojos queridos
mirándome
a través de la ausencia.
Tus ojos tan vitales,
en tus últimos días apagados,
tristes, mudos,
que me miraban en silencio,
anegándome el alma
de contenidas lágrimas.

THERE, BY THE BED

There, by the bed,
are your glasses.
Their lenses are empty
two lakes without shores.
Absorbed, contemplative,
I take them in my hands.
Your eyes are behind them,
I feel your eyes,
looking, looking, looking,
and I tenderly rest them
on my breast,
as though it were your head.
I kiss them.
They are your dear eyes
gazing at me
through the emptiness.
Your lovely, lively eyes,
so dim in your final days,
saddened, muted,
watching me in silence,
flooding my soul
with pent-up tears.

Versos y Estampas

Sketches and Verses

I

HOY la tarde era serena, con un sol de oro; y mañana igual, todo el verano y sus días. Y, ¿qué juego hacemos hoy? Se oían los nombres en distintas voces y corríamos llevando de la mano a todas las niñas para formar un corro muy grande. Comenzaba el juego, siempre, con una niña en el centro del corro. Y empezábamos a girar lentamente, con una ligera ondulación. Pasaba la rueda sobre el mar. Ahora azul, ahora rosa, ahora blanca, como un pequeño arco-iris. La voz delgada, infantil, se perdía entre las manos enlazadas. Y el mar y la tarde se tornaban rosas, sobre las cabezas y en los pies descalzos de todas las niñas.

I

SOBRE la superficie
del mar encandilado
de las seis de la tarde,
saltan algunos peces
que dejan sobre el agua,
al caer, una onda.

Así, a trechos, bordado
el mar por esta aguja
parece que sonríe:
sonrisas que se ensanchan
y cierran lentamente;
sonreír de la orilla,
encaje de la falda
azul y transparente.

I

TODAY the afternoon was serene, with a sun of gold; tomorrow—
the same, every day, all summer long. So, what game would we
play? We heard names called out clearly, and hurried to pull the
other children by the hand into a very large circle. The game be-
gan with a little girl in the center. Then the circle would start to
turn slowly, undulating lightly. The wheel passed over the sea.
Now blue, now pink, now white, like a small rainbow. The deli-
cate childlike voice was lost among the clasped hands. The sea
and the afternoon turned to roses, over the heads and the bare
feet of all the little girls.

I

OVER the surface
of the incandescent sea
at six in the evening,
fish leap, and on falling
ripple the water.

Embroidered at intervals
by this needle, the ocean
looks as if it were smiling:
each of the smiles widening
and then closing slowly;
smiling from the shore,
lacework on a skirt
sky-blue and transparent.

II

ESTE perro negro y grande, ¡cuánto nos hizo sufrir! Nos lo encontrábamos, siempre, en nuestros juegos de escondite y en nuestras carreras por la arena. Llegaba corriendo, amenazador, con la lengua larga y roja entre los colmillos afilados. Nos dispersábamos dando gritos, buscando un refugio. El perro nos seguía. Una tarde, nos buscó inútilmente por la playa. Yo lo observaba desde la ventana. Me habían prohibido salir. En la playa no había nadie. El perro buscó largo rato y se echó a dormir, por último. Aquella tarde me hubiera sentado a su lado.

2

El murmullo de la playa
entra a oscuras
por la ventana cerrada,
entre las maderas
verdes, apretadas.
Y se llena la estancia
de olor de arena húmeda,
de mar y de luna blanca.

II

THAT big black dog, how he made us suffer! We were always bumping into him during our games of hide and seek, as we ran along the sand. He'd come running up to us, menacing, his long red tongue between sharp fangs. We'd scatter, screaming, seeking refuge. The dog chased us. One afternoon, he searched in vain for us along the beach. I watched him from my window. I'd been forbidden to go outside. There was no one on the beach. The dog searched for a long while and then finally lay down to sleep. That afternoon I would have gladly stayed at his side.

2

THE murmur of the beach
enters in the dark
through the closed window,
through the looming
green forest.
The living room is filled
with the odor of damp sand,
the sea and the white moon.

III

DESPUÉS de cenar, nos paseábamos por la acera húmeda, salitrosa del aliento del mar, hasta la esquina. Yo le decía: «papá, ¿por qué no llamas al chiquillo?» Y papá gritaba: «¡chiquillo!» Y el eco repetía: «¡chi-qui-llo!» ¡Cómo gozaba yo entonces! y gritaba: «ven», y el eco, «ven»; yo después, «bo-bo», y se oía, «bo-bo». Entonces me reía nerviosa, algo asustada, y, lejos, «el chiquillo» se reía también.

Yo lo imaginaba moreno por el sol, medio desnudo, escondido detrás de las maderas de alguno de aquellos portales marineros que exhalaban a la media tarde el olor recogido de la pesca. Dos o tres veces he llegado esta noche hasta la esquina en el ir y venir del paseo. Tengo un deseo de gritar: «¡Chiquillo, ven, bobo!» Pero tengo miedo de matarlo.

3

QUÉ desconsuelo tener
el corazón tan incierto
sin saber—mi cieguecito—
por dónde andas tan ciego.
Qué desconsuelo escuchar
el corazón a destiempo:
unas veces tan deprisa
y otras, a veces, tan lento.
Yo no quisiera tener
el corazón tan incierto,
pues se me hace pequeñito
y se esconde muy adentro
como un reloj que no anda
y ándame loco en el pecho.

AFTER dinner, salty from the breath of the sea, we would walk along the wet sidewalk, to the corner. I would say to him, *Papa, why don't you call Chiquillo?* And father would call out, *Chiquillo!*, and the echo would repeat *Chi-qui-llo!* How I enjoyed that! And I would call out, *Come!*, and hear the echo, *Come!* Then later, *Bo-bo*, and *Bo-bo* was heard. Then I would laugh nervously, a bit frightened, and, far away, *Chiquillo* also laughed.

I imagined him browned by the sun, half-naked, hidden behind the woods of those docks that exhale the midafternoon odor of the day's catch. Once or twice on that particular night when I got to the corner in my meandering walk, I had the urge to call out: *Chiquillo, Come, Bobo!* But I was afraid by calling out I might somehow cause his death.

3

HOW disconcerting to have
a heart so uncertain
without knowing—my little blind one—
where you wander so blindly.
How disconcerting to listen
to an uneven heart:
beating too fast at times,
and other times, too slow.
I don't want a heart
that beats so uncertainly,
since it makes me feel small
and hides very deep
like a clock that won't run
and drives my chest crazy.

IV

ESTA caja de cartón llena de figurines recortados, al encontrarla
hoy de nuevo, y al abrirla, me ha llenado el alma de recuerdos.
Dentro, unas sobre otras, en mezcla de tonos desteñidos, he
vuelto a ver a todas mis amigas: mis señoritas de papel. Todas
tenían su historia de amor: un amor blanco, de papel, como la
nube sobre la azotea. Allí, arriba, el cuarto pequeño con la puerta
abierta frente al limonero de la casa vecina y el risco poblado de
casitas de colores y gritos lejanos. Aquí, mis historias. Cierro la
caja de cartón. ¡Adiós mis amigas!

4

EL sol en la playa tiene
juegos de niño pequeño
con el mar y las sombrillas.
Juego incierto y un correr
de prisa
de una a la otra
esquina.
Y una nube que pasa, blanca,
para dar sombra a la playa
dormida
y apagar el azul y el rojo
de las caras
bajo la cretona de la sombrilla.

THIS cardboard box full of short figurines—finding it again to-day, and opening it, my soul filled with memories. Inside, one on top of the other, in a mixture of faded shades of color, I have come to see all of my women friends, my little ladies of paper. Each one has her love story: a white love, of paper, like the cloud over the flat roof. There, upstairs, the small room with the open door facing the lemon tree of the house next door and the cliff peopled with colorful houses and distant cries. . . . Here, my stories. I close the box. Goodbye friends!

4

THE sun on the beach
like a small child
plays with its toys,
the sea and the parasols.
An uncertain game of running
hurriedly
from one corner
to the other.
Then a passing white cloud
darkens the slumbering
beach,
softening the blue and red
of the faces
under the linen of the parasol.

DESDE la esquina bajábamos al muro, corriendo, y saltábamos ligeras, unas tras otras, volviendo a subir y a saltar. Una voz, de vez en cuando, gritaba: ‹‹¡cuidado; se van a hacer daño!›› Pero no hacíamos caso. Al saltar nos gustaba mucho ver flotar en el aire los encajes y los vuelos de los delantales como alas de mariposa. Una tarde, al saltar, una de las pequeñas se hizo daño en un pie. Al ver la sangre en la sandalia blanca nos unimos todas temblorosas. La pequeña se asustó y comenzó a llorar. Desde aquel día nos prohibieron ese juego, y pasábamos ante el muro deprisa para no caer en la tentación.

Esta tarde contemplo el muro pequeño, donde saltaron tantas veces mis siete años de tira bordada. Y siento un hondo desconsuelo de no poder saltar ahora, y mi pensamiento está saltando por el muro.

5

EL viento trae todo el rumor
por el camino arriba.
Tú subes con el viento
dentro de mí,
en mi ensueño,
lejos y cerca,
distinto y el mismo.
Yo te espero
esta tarde
—claridad dormida—,
y el viento trae
todo el rumor,
el mismo y distinto.

V

AT the corner, we hopped down from the wall, running, skipping, one after the other, turning to climb back up and jump down again. From time to time, a voice cried out, *Be careful, you'll hurt yourselves!* But we paid no attention. Jumping down, we delighted in seeing lace floating in the air, and petticoats flying up like butterfly wings. One afternoon, one of the small girls hurt her foot jumping. When we saw the blood on her white sandal, we all crowded together, trembling. She was frightened and began to cry. From that day on, the jumping game has been forbidden, and we hurry past that wall in order not to be tempted to play there.

This afternoon I think about that little wall, and the many times my seven years of embroidered cloth jumped down from it. I am unhappy that I can't jump down right now, as my thoughts skip along the wall.

5

THE wind brings its whispers
through the upper street.
You rise with the wind
inside me,
in my dreams,
nearby yet far away,
distinct and the same . . .
I wait for you
this afternoon
—sleeping clarity—,
until the wind returns
with its usual, yet always different
whispers.

AQUEL día estaba yo en la acera, bajo la ventana, y la muchacha asomada en ella. Luego llegó él y me acarició la cara. Las niñas hacían unos hoyos grandes en la playa, y venía el mar y se los llenaba de agua y piedrecitas. Una nube grande se puso sobre la playa. Ella y él hablaban muy bajo. Yo, de cuando en cuando, levantaba los ojos y les miraba en silencio. Después hablaron un poco más alto. En la playa hicieron una montaña alta, y saltaron los niños. Luego la rompieron gritando. Los dos se callaron. Yo cogí un palito y me puse a hacer letras en la acera. Luego él dijo algo y ella bajó los ojos. Luego hubo un largo silencio. Él se llevó la mano a la frente, distraído, y se fué. Ella cerró la ventana. Entonces yo bajé a la orilla del mar a buscar vidrios de colores.

6

AGUA clara del estanque.
Era un espejo del chopo
y alfombra verde del cielo
con reflejos de los árboles.
¡Oh, si yo hubiera podido
entrar con los pies descalzos
y ser el viento en el agua
y hacer agitar el chopo!

THAT day I was on the sidewalk, beneath the window where the girl sat looking out. He arrived later and stroked my cheek. The children were digging holes in the sand, which the sea came and filled with water and tiny pebbles. A big cloud appeared over the beach. She and he talked very softly. From time to time I raised my eyes and looked at them in silence. Later they talked more loudly. On the beach the children made a tall mountain, and then jumped off of it. Later, they laughed as they destroyed it. The couple stopped talking. I took a stick and started to print letters in the packed dirt of the pathway. Then he said something, and she lowered her eyes. There was a long silence. Sadly he put his hand to his forehead and left. She closed the window. I went down to the beach, to look for bits of colored glass.

6

CLEAR water of the pool.
You were the mirror of the poplar
and the green carpet of the sky
with reflections of the trees.
Oh! If I had been able
to enter barefooted,
to be the wind on the water
and make the poplar quake!

VII

COMO era al amanecer, me dejaron acostada y fueron todos a recibirles. Llegaban los padres y la hermana después de aquel viaje tan largo. Y yo iba a ver a «mama», a «papa».... Yo no los recordaba. Toda mi fantasía vagaba oscura en derredor y no podía dormir. Se oyó primero el rodar de un coche. Luego unas voces que se acercaban y el patio se llenó de besos. Y ahora, en la escalera, un tintineo de cascabeles. Y la cabeza se me desvaneció. ¡Qué alegre era la llegada! Se abrió la puerta de mi cuarto y entraron dos señoras con los brazos abiertos. Sentí que me besaban, me abrazaban, y estuve unos momentos ahogada entre pieles húmedas y en el perfume cálido de las mejillas y los labios. Y luego, otros ojos de un señor que me miraba, brillándole uno detrás de un cristal, y una mano que me acariciaba la cabeza. Y como alguien dijo que yo sabía leer todos salieron apresurados en busca de un periódico. Y yo leí: FESTIVIDAD DEL DÍA.

1

LA noche trajo a la luna
sobre la playa y el mar,
y las rocas se adornaron
con su brillo, humedecidas.
Yo le contaba a mi niño
—no se quería dormir—
que la luna era una reina
de jazmín
que salía por las noches
con su regador de plata
para regar su jardín.

¡El mar, el mar, y mi niño
que no se quería dormir!

As it was dawn, they let me sleep and went to receive my parents and sister, who were arriving after a very long voyage. And I was going to get to see my *mama* and *papa*. . . . I did not remember them. All my fantasy wandered darkly in the hall and I could not sleep. First the wheels of a carriage were heard. Later, voices that came nearer, and the patio was filled with kisses. Then, on the stairs, a tinkling of bells. I was beside myself. The arrival—what happiness! The door of my room opened, and two women with open arms came in. I felt them kissing me, embracing me, and for a few moments I was smothered between humid skin and hot perfume of cheeks and lips. Later, other eyes looked at me, a man's eyes, one shining behind a crystal. A hand stroked my head. Someone said that I knew how to read, and everyone ran out to look for a newspaper. I read: TODAY'S FESTIVITIES.

1

THE night brought the moon
over the beach and the sea,
and the rocks, splashed with water,
adorned themselves
with its brilliance.
I told my child
(who didn't want to go to sleep)
that the moon
was a jasmine queen,
and she came out at night
with a sprinkler of silver
to water the garden.

The sea, the sea, and my son
who didn't want to sleep!

HAY un loco en la playa. Es un niño, un muchacho pequeño.
Nosotros le llamamos «el loco». Este niño era el terror de los que
jugábamos a la orilla del mar. Nos tiraba piedrecitas desde lejos y
gritaba con una voz extraordinaria. A nosotros nos daba mucho
miedo. Algunos días no le veíamos en toda la mañana, pero, por
la tarde, cuando no había ni sol ni mar, aparecían por entre unos
mariscos en montaña los ojos brillantes y la cara moderna del
muchacho. Entonces, todos los pequeños nos escondíamos en
casa y no volvíamos a salir.

He visto al «loco» hace unas tardes. Me ha reconocido con sus
ojos grandes de llama encendida. Estuvo sentado largo rato en la
playa, escarbando la arena donde llegaba el mar de vez en cuando.

8

SOBRE la plaza brillante
de lluvia
vierte la sombra de sus hojas
un árbol
que a la luna recoge
en sus hojas
y cuelga gracioso
en sus ramas.
(La plaza oscurecida alrededor
de la hoguera romántica).

Los cristales de mi ventana lloran
lágrimas y lágrimas . . .
Yo, que contemplo la noche,
también lloro, infinitas, mis lágrimas.
(Pero al dejar la noche he sonreído:
«es la lluvia», le he dicho a mi alma).

THERE was a crazy person on the beach. He was a child, a small boy. We call him *el loco*. This child was a terror to those of us who played on the seashore. He threw stones at us from afar and yelled with an extraordinary voice, frightening us. Some days we wouldn't see him all morning, but, in the afternoon, when there was neither sun nor sea, those flashing eyes and the startling face appeared from behind mountains of seashells. Then all of us who were small hid ourselves away in our houses, and didn't go out again.

I saw *el loco* some afternoons back. Those large smoldering eyes recognized me. He sat for a long time on the beach, scraping the sand that the sea reached from time to time.

8

OVER the brilliant plaza
of rain
a tree casts the shadow
of its leaves,
gathers the moon
into those leaves
and hangs it graciously
from its branches.
(The plaza grows dark around
the romantic hearth).

My windowpanes cry
tears and tears . . .
I, who contemplate the night,
also cry infinite tears.
(As I left the night I smiled:
It's the rain, I said to my soul).

S E sentaba cerca de nosotros y nos miraba con sus ojillos grises, desconsolados. Hacía tiempo que lo notábamos, pero ninguna le hacíamos caso. Aquella tarde construyó cerca de nosotros, casi a nuestro lado, una linda casa de arena, más linda que las nuestras, y todas la mirábamos con recelo. Y de pronto, un pie decidido la echó abajo. Nos miró desconsoladamente. Entonces la acariciamos. Ella alzó los ojos, como cenizas mojadas, sonriendo. Vino ya todas las tardes y se sentaba cerca de nosotras. Al principio, llevaba un traje desteñido y sucio, mal peinada y descalza. Pero una tarde vino con sus alpargatas y el traje lavado, y se acercó más y nos cogió las manos. Aquel día se había peinado en dos trenzas y estuvo toda la tarde silenciosa. Cuando se fue me dijo, como una explicación: ¡Me gustan tanto los lazos en la trenza! Y al día siguiente le llevé uno de regalo, dentro de una caja. Cuando nos despedimos, al fin de verano, usaba medias y zapatos negros. Hoy ya es una mujer. La he visto anoche sentada en un banco de piedra del muelle, en silencio, y toda la ceniza de sus ojos brillaba encendida.

9

E L hilo de agua, rizado,
sube y se abre en lo alto;
luego se pierde en el agua
temblorosa con su fondo
de sol, tembloroso y blanco.
El pecho se alza. Un suspiro
todo luz se va en el aire.
Vivo, el ciprés se ilumina
entre los rosales blancos.

S H E sat nearby and looked at us with her small grey disconsolate eyes. We had noticed her around for a long time, but didn't pay her any particular attention. That afternoon, nearby, almost right beside us, she built a beautiful sand castle, more beautiful than ours, and we all looked at it with envy. Suddenly, one sure kick knocked it down. She looked at us dejectedly. From that moment we became affectionate with her. She raised those eyes that had the look of wet ashes and smiled. Every afternoon after that, she came and sat next to us. In the beginning, she wore a dirty and stained dress, her hair was unkempt, and she was barefoot. But one afternoon she showed up wearing sandals and a clean dress, and she came closer and took our hands. That day she had combed her hair, and she was silent all afternoon. When she left she said to me, as if by explanation, *I like bows in my tresses so much!* The following day I brought her a gift, in a box. When we said goodbye, at the end of summer, she was wearing stockings and black shoes. Today she's a woman. I saw her last night seated on a stone bench along the dock, silent, the ashes of her eyes glowing like fire.

9

T H E thread of water, curled,
rises and opens on high;
later it is lost in the trembling
water with its depth of sun,
trembling and white.
My chest rises. A sigh
all light escapes into the air.
Alive, the cypress is illuminated
through white rosebushes.

X

CUANDO el carnaval se acercaba, todos vivíamos en un continuo repasar los días: uno, dos, tres, cuatro, hasta el día señalado. Nos hablábamos en silencio, misteriosamente. Ya en la víspera, nos mirábamos temblorosos, deseando gritar, dar saltos, pero recogidos en el deseo. Nos acostaban muy temprano, después de preparar el disfraz sobre una silla, y nos dormíamos muy tarde, con un sueño agitado, lleno de saltos de carnaval. Y a la mañana, después de vestirnos con nuestros disfraces, bajábamos al patio húmedo de la noche y empezábamos a llamar con unas voces delgadas, embrujadas. Venía la abuela fingiendo un asombro asustado en sus ojos y nos decía: «Pasen, pasen, mascaritas»; y pasábamos todos muy serios. Y mamá llegaba y se asustaba mucho también. Y como nos daba mucha pena—un miedo de uno mismo, interiormente—tirábamos el antifaz y le decíamos: «¡Si soy yo»! Y toda la mañana se colgaba de sorpresas.

10

MIS dolores se escondían
en el fondo de mi alma.
Eran tantos, tan pequeños,
que casi no me molestaban.

Los guardaba con amor
en el fondo de mi alma.

As carnival approached, we lived in a continuous counting of the days: one, two, three, four until the day arrived. We talked to each other quietly, mysteriously. The night before, we looked at each other trembling with excitement, wanting to scream, leap, but subdued our desire. We went to bed early, after draping our costumes over a chair, and slept late, in agitated sleep, full of all the excitement of carnival. In the morning, after putting on our disguises, we went down to the patio, still wet with the dew, and began to call out with delicate and witchy voices. Grandmother would come affecting astonishing fright in her eyes, and say to us *Come along, come along little masks* . . . and we all passed by very seriously. Mother arrived, very frightened also. And as we couldn't stand it—we were scared of our own shadows—we threw off the masks and said to her: *It's me!* The whole morning was hung with surprises.

10

My bits of grief hide themselves
in the depths of my soul.
They are so numerous, so small,
they hardly bother me.

I watch over them with love
in the depths of my soul.

ERA un viejecito. Venía todos los sábados a recoger su limosna y se sentaba al final de la escalera. Nosotros, desde por la mañana, pedíamos para él su peseta, y toda la tarde le esperábamos queriéndole reconocer en cada llamada. Nos traía siempre estampas. Revolvía no sabíamos dónde, en todos los rincones; buscaba, buscaba y nos traía estampas. Llegaban a nuestras manos casi rotas, pero nosotros las cogíamos y las guardábamos en una cajita. Nos daba siempre un beso en la mano con sus labios temblorosos de viejo, arrodillado en el suelo, con los brazos cruzados ante toda la luz que entraba por la puerta, como un Cristo en un marco de plata, y luego se iba apoyado en un palo, un palo torcido que le torcía el andar. Antonio, le llamábamos. Un día se le llamó en broma, ¡Antonio!, y él volvió los ojos bañados de sombras para contestarnos. Y todos reímos comentando el caso. ¡Pues era curioso!

Aquel sábado le esperábamos y vino la noche sin que llegara el viejo. Y cuando nos dormían, alguien dijo: «Hoy no ha venido Antonio». Y se inició una risa, y una explicación acerca del nombre, que murió apagada en una voz soñolienta. Y Antonio no volvió más. Nunca. Luego oímos hablar de un asilo, de los pobres que piden limosna. No comprendimos nada.

II

REZABA la lluvia
su oración del alba:
iba desgranando
las cuentas menudas
del blanco rosario.
Yo las recogía
dentro de mis manos,
y también rezaba
junto con la lluvia
mi oración del alba.

H E was a diminutive old man. He came every Saturday to get his alms, and sat down at the foot of the stairs. Since morning, we had been begging for a *peseta* to give him, so all afternoon we expected him to be at our every beck and call. He always brought us stamps. He went through things in nooks and crannies unknown to us, searching here and there in every corner, until he found stamps to bring to us. They came into our hands almost destroyed, but we accepted them and kept them in a little box. He always kissed us on the hand with his tremulous old man's lips, kneeling on the ground with his arms crossed before all the light that came through the door, like a Christ in a silver picture frame. Later he went away leaning on his stick, a twisted stick which he turned as he walked. Among ourselves we called him Antonio. One day in jest we called out, *Antonio!* and he turned his eyes bathed in shadows to answer us. And we all laughed, commenting on that occurrence. It was so strange!

That particular Saturday we waited for him, but night came without the old man showing up. And when we were being put to bed, someone said, *Antonio didn't come today.* That caused laughter, and an explanation about the name, that died in a sleepy voice. Antonio never returned. Never. Later we heard talk of an asylum for beggars. We understood none of it.

II

T H E rain prayed
its prayer of dawn:
shelling
the tiny beads
from the white rosary.
And I gathered them up
in my hands,
and also prayed
with the rain
my prayer of dawn.

AQUELLA mañana blanca, ¡cómo la recuerdo! Nos habíamos levantado un poco más tarde que otros días, después de haber estado unos momentos con el sopor del último sueño, percibiendo de cuando en cuando, al abrirse los ojos, los barrotes de las camitas que parecían jaulas de hierro. Nos pusieron unos delantales largos, anchos, que se nos escurrían por todo el cuerpo, y nos empujaron al patio. El patio estaba frío, brillante de las primeras horas de la mañana y verde de enredaderas. A un tiempo todos hicimos la misma pregunta: ‹‹Y la niña, ¿cómo está?›› Nadie respondió. En el comedor nos esperaban las tazas humeantes del café con leche, y el pan y la manteca. La mano que nos guiaba estaba muy pálida. Alguien dijo, de pronto: ‹‹Los niños, que los lleven arriba››. Y subimos todos, despacio, en silencio. ¡Qué larga, qué penosa nos pareció la escalera! Y no tuvieron que darnos la noticia. Cuando entramos en ya alcoba la llevábamos el corazón lleno de flores, y los ojos llorosos. Sobre la cama ancha, blanca de rosas, había una caja de muñecas también blanca. Y luego se la llevaron. Desde la baranda del corredor la vimos cruzar por el patio, bajo la enredadera, a través de las lágrimas. Y ya no la vimos más. Quedó temblando entre las flores, en el aire, la sombra blanca de la caja toda la mañana.

Y otra mañana estábamos en el muro de piedra y nos llegó en el aire el eco de una queja, y todos nos miramos en silencio, temblorosos. Pero llegó la hermana y nos dijo: ‹‹Es que se arrullan las palomas blancas››, y todos quedamos consternados, mirándolas ahora revolotear en la azotea. Y un día, cuando jugábamos gritando en el cuarto grande, nos hicieron salir uno a uno, y nos separaron silenciosamente. A la noche aquella nos dijeron: ‹‹Sabes, la abuelita se ha muerto››. Y toda la casa se llenó de gente. Y la mañana nos despertó la queja lejana de las palomas blancas, y todos se levantaron aturdidos, presurosos.

THAT white morning long ago. . . . How well I remember it! We had gotten up a little later than on other days, and after having spent a few moments in the lethargy of our last dream, perceiving from time to time, upon opening our eyes, that the bars of our little beds seemed like steel cages. They brought out long and ample smocks, slipped them over our bodies, and pushed us out onto the patio. The patio was cold, brilliant in the first hours of the day, and green with its surrounding climbing vines. All at once we all asked the same question: *And the little girl, how is she?* No one responded. In the dining room steaming cups of café au lait awaited us, and bread and butter. The hand that guided us was very pallid. Someone said, suddenly: *The children, bring them up.* And we all went up, slowly, in silence. How long and difficult the stairs seemed to us. They didn't have to tell us. When we entered the bedroom, our hearts were already full of sadness, our eyes full of tears. On the wide bed, white with roses, there was a white box for dolls. Later they took it away. From the hall veranda we saw it cross the patio, and more. There all morning, trembling among the flowers, in the air, was the white shadow of the box.

On a similar morning, at the stone wall, an echo of complaint came to us on the air, and we all looked at each other in silence, trembling. But our sister arrived and said to us: *It's only the white doves cooing.* But we remained confused, as we watched them wheel over the flat roof. Another day, when we were playing and yelling in the big room, they made us leave one by one, and separated us silently. That night they said: *You should all know, grandma has died.* The house filled with people. In the morning the distant complaint of the doves woke us, and we all got up hurriedly and confused.

No te acerques al estanque:
antes me he mirado en él
y vi su fondo a través
de mi sombra. No te acerques
al estanque:
tendrás el pecho hondo y frío
y tembloroso del agua.

12

DON'T go near the pool—
earlier I saw myself in it
and through my shadow
its depths. *Don't go near
the pool:*
it will make
your heart deep and cold
and as tremulous as water.

COMO así lo habían mandado los padres de Inglaterra, así se lo pusieron. Era un día de paseo, y para que el niño fuese guapo le pusieron el abrigo. Los demás le mirábamos engalanarse, abrigados en los nuestros de confección isleña. Cuando se lo hubo puesto, le observaron unos instantes en silencio. El niño dio unas vueltas en el cuarto, tropezando, con el abrigo colgado de los hombros. Se hizo una observación en voz baja: ‹‹¿No lo encuentras demasiado largo››? Y otra: ‹‹Debe de ser de moda››. Y salimos de paseo. Paseamos mucho y la gente nos miraba, nos miraba y sonreía: una sonrisa larga, muy larga, como el abrigo. Cuando regresamos a casa el niño preguntó: ‹‹¿Por qué me miraban tanto››? Y la tía le dijo: ‹‹Porque llevas un abrigo de Londres, porque es muy elegante››. Y se acostó con aquella ilusión. ¡Cuando se enteraron los padres! Aún hoy, recordando esta anécdota, nos sonreímos todos. El niño es ya un hombre que se ríe a carcajadas, mientras la tía le acaricia la cabeza con una pena que se esconde entre los pliegues de aquel abrigo.

13

SOBRE el mar, bajo el cielo, blancas, densas,
vienen todas las velas desplegadas
en el aire, dorado y transparente.
Y en la proa, delgada como brisa,
la corona de espuma alborotada
es adorno rizado de su frente.

En la playa, de oros soleada,
las mujeres esperan a las barcas
con los ojos al mar, intensamente.
Y en el ramo de velas olorosas
—brisa de mar, aroma de mariscos—
hay un anhelo cálido y creciente.

XIII

JUST because the parents had it sent from England, they put it on him. It was a day of walking around, and so in an attempt to make the little boy look handsome they put the overcoat on him. The rest of us looked at him, all dressed up, while we were wrapped in coats made on the island. Once he had it on, they looked him over for some minutes in silence. The child took a couple of turns around the room, stumbling, with the coat on his shoulders. An observation was made in a soft voice: *Don't you think it's a bit long?* And another: *Must be the style.* We went out walking. We walked around for quite a while and the people looked at us and smiled, a very long smile, like the coat. When we returned home, the little boy asked: *Why were they looking at me so much?* An aunt said to him: *Because you were wearing a coat from London,* because it's very elegant. And he went to bed with that illusion. How delighted my parents were! Even today, thinking of this anecdote, we all laugh. By now the boy is a grown man who guffaws, while the aunt caresses his head, with grief that is hidden in the folds of that coat.

13

OVER the sea, under the sky,
come all the dense white sails
unfurled in the air, golden and transparent.
And in the prow, thin as a breeze,
the noisy crown of foam
a curly adornment of its bow.

On the beach, as bright as golden coins,
the women wait for the boats,
their eyes intent on the sea.
And in the arm of aromatic sails
—sea breeze, aroma of mollusks—
there is desire, hot and swelling.

¡Cuánto diera por ver llegar un día
la barca con la blanca vela al viento
con rumbo hacia la orilla, desrizada;
y en pie en la proa —tijera de los mares—
a ti, todos mis sueños, presentido
con el azul del mar en la mirada!

What I would give to see my ship
arrive some day, with its white sails unfurled
before the wind, bound for the shore;
and standing on the prow—that cuts the seas
like scissors—you, all my dreams, as predicted,
with the blue of the sea in your look!

¡CUÁNTO le hemos temido también! No salíamos solos, en la casa de campo, hasta la muralla, por miedo a encontrarlo. Primero se oía de lejos, muy lejos, el zumbido ronco de sus alaridos. Toda la montaña temblaba, redonda del eco de su voz, y los árboles sacudían las hojas secas. Es mudo este viejo. Aquel llorar de su garganta seca, y el chasquido de la lengua contra el paladar, nos aterrorizaba. Llegaba corriendo por el camino alto, saltándole el buche de la camisa repleta de pan, pan duro y pan blando, y daba unos gritos para anunciar su llegada. Salían los criados y nosotros detrás, escondiéndonos. Le decían: «Baila, baila un poco». Él daba unos saltos grotescos, deshechos en jirones de tela y en el chocar del pan dentro de la camisa. Luego le daban un cigarro, diez céntimos, y aullaba, gritaba de nuevo y huía saltando por entre las matas. A la noche dormía abajo, junto a la bodega, y a la madrugada salía a los campos oliéndole el traje a uva madura.

14

MI camino tiene una luz,
—hay un pajarito cantando en un pino—.
Voy caminando hacia la luz,
—hay una ranita cantando en la acequia—.
Me acerco y se agranda la luz,
—hay una chiquilla cantando en la fuente—.
¿Adónde me lleva esta luz?
—Hay un lucerito cantando en la noche—.
¡Me prende en su fuego la luz!
—Hay una voz nueva cantando a mi oído—.

How afraid we were of him! We wouldn't go out alone at our country house, wouldn't go as far as the wall for fear of bumping into him. First he was heard from very far away, the hoarse buzzing of his hew and cry. The whole mountain trembled, surrounded by the echo of his voice, and the trees shook off their dry leaves. He can't talk, that old man. That crying from his dry throat, the clicking of his tongue against his palate, terrorized us. He arrived at a run, shirttails coming out of his pants, replete with hard and soft bread. He cried out to announce his arrival. The servants went out to look, and we hid behind them. They said to him: *Dance, do a little dance.* He would make a few grotesque leaps, destroyed in twirls of cloth and the bread knocking around in his shirt. Later they gave him a cigarette, ten centimes, and he howled, screaming again and leaping in flight through the shrubbery. At night he slept below, next to the shed, and at dawn he left for the fields, his clothes smelling of ripe grapes.

14

My road has a light—
there's a small bird singing in the pines.
I'm walking toward that light—
there is a little frog singing in the swamp.
I get closer and the light gets bigger—
there's a cricket singing in the fountain.
Where does this light take me?
There's an insect singing in the night.
Will I catch on fire from the light?
There's a new voice singing in my ear.

Es mi recuerdo más turbio, el que más me cuesta aclarar. No puedo recordar bien cómo era Rosa. ¿Alta, baja? Una niña de unos siete o nueve años, sucia y despeinada. Surgía del café entre el humo rosado de nuestros cantos, cuando hacíamos el corro en la plaza de San Bernardo. Su aparición nos recordaba al Simón Cirineo. Andaba sobre el lado derecho, con una suave curva en el izquierdo, llevando un pequeño, tan sucio como ella, jinete en su cadera flexible. Cuando cantábamos la canción de ‹‹el vestidito››, lo dejaba sentado en el suelo, apoyado contra la pared desteñida del café, en éxtasis de admiración, y se ponía también a cantar, sin ton ni son. ¿Por qué cuando decía ‹‹cortito de alante, larguito de atrás›› su voz se llenaba de más vibraciones? Su voz era segura como el pregón de un heraldo y la envolvía toda, toda, y la dejaba más sucia y más descosida. ¡Ya está ahí Rosa la del Café! ¡Oh, recuerdo empañado, luz débil de mis años, empequeñecida por otra luz más fuerte! ¿Dónde está Rosa? ¿Qué ha sido de Rosa y de su cruz de carne? Cuando pienso que acaso la conozco, que acaso la he visto pasar alguna vez, siento deseos de salir a la calle, y de murmurar a todas las muchacas risueñas que pasan por mi lado: ¡Rosa la del Café!

15

ToDA mi ilusión la he puesto
en la espera de una mañana.
¿Cómo vendrás? ¿Adornado
de blanca flor de retama
o de flor de pensamiento
que de luto se engalana?
¿Vendrás con rojas miradas
o con pálidas miradas?
¿Tendrás voz, tendrás sonrisa,
o no me guardarás nada?

IT is my most confused memory, the one that's hardest for me to clear up. I don't remember very well what Rosa was like. Short? Tall? A little girl of six or nine, who was dirty and whose hair was never combed. She came out of the café into the rosy smoke of our songs, when we gathered our circle of friends in the Plaza of San Bernardo. Her appearance reminded us of Simón Cirineo. She leaned to the right when she walked, her body curved smoothly back to the left, carrying a small horseman on her flexible hip that was as dirty as she was. When we sang *The Little Dress*, she left the little horseman leaned up against the stained wall of the café, in an ecstasy of admiration, and also began to sing, out of tune. Why, when we sang *short in the front, long in back* was her voice so full of vibratos? Her voice was as steady as the announcement of a herald, and it surrounded her totally, leaving her dirtier and more ragged. There's Rosa of the Café! Oh, dim memory, weak light of my years, made small by another stronger light! Where is Rosa? What has happened to Rosa and her crucifix of flesh? When I think that I hardly knew her, that I barely saw her pass by once, I want to go out into the street, and whisper to all the smiling little girls that pass by me: Rosa of the Café!

15

I have placed all of my illusions
in expectation of a tomorrow.
How will you come? Adorned
in the white flower of the furze
or the flower of thought
which drapes itself in mourning?
Will you come with red glances
or white ones?
Will you have a voice, smile,
or will you look at me at all?

¡Mañana, horizonte en niebla,
fiel timón de mi fragata:
hace tiempo que me llegas
con las velas desplegadas!

Tomorrow, clouded horizon,
faithful tiller of my frigate:
you have been a long time coming
with unfurled sails!

LA última noche del año, después de comer, todos salían y nos quedábamos las dos solas con la antigua sirvienta. (Antes de marcharse nos dejaban, para entrar el año, unos refrescos y unos dulces.) Y les veíamos salir al baile muy contentos, en espera del Año Nuevo. Nos sentábamos alrededor de la mesa. La vieja trabajando su encaje—maravilla de hojas y flores entre las manos—, y nosotras hablando y riendo. ¡Qué valientes nos encontrábamos al ver pasar las horas en el reloj! ¡Cerca ya de las doce, el encaje se mustiaba entre las manos y la charla y las risas se envolvían en una niebla espesa de sueño! ¡Se llenaban los vasos poco a poco, en un medio silencio, y se esperaba ya con impaciencia la campanada del reloj! ¡Tan, tan, tan! Había un murmullo de alegría despertada; un bostezo interrumpido. Luego el sueño indomable que nos arrastraba a las alcobas. Y quedaban los vasos sobre la mesa, apenas empezados. Luego los pasos cansados de la vieja y su voz de niña que decía: «Hasta mañanita». Y todo tenía el sopor de un sueño viejo.

16

MIS pies descalzos, de plata.
La orilla muerta del mar
en la playa,
sobre el sudario de arena
mojada.
La noche viuda, enlutada,
se cubre toda de lágrimas.
La luna, mis pies descalzos
de plata, dentro del agua.

THE last night of the year, after dinner, they all went out and just the two of us remained with the ancient servant. (Before leaving they put out drinks and sweets for us, with which to bring in the New Year.) We saw them leave for the dance very contented, as we awaited the New Year. We sat around the table. The old one tatting her lace—a marvel of leaves and flowers in her hands—while we chatted and laughed. How brave we seemed watching the hours pass on the clock! Around midnight the lace languished in her hands, and the chatting and laughing were turned into a thick fog of sleepiness. The glasses were filled slowly, in silence, as we waited with impatience for the striking of the clock! Ding! ding, ding! There was a murmur of awakened joy; an interrupted yawn. Later indomitable sleep drew us toward our bedrooms. On the table, the glasses scarcely touched . . . Later the tired steps of the old one and her child's voice that said: *See you bright and early in the morning.* It all had the lethargy of an old dream.

16

MY bare feet, of silver.
The dead shore of the sea
on the beach,
over the shroud of wet
sand.
The widowed night, in mourning,
is totally covered with tears.
The moon, my bare feet
of silver, in the water.

DE nuevo ante la ventana
sola con el horizonte.
La tarde vuelve y se va,
aeronave de su ensueño.
Todo va de cerca a lejos.
Nada se sienta a su lado.
El mar hace lentejuelas
en su pandero amarillo.
Nada se quedó olvidado:
ni un pañolito de seda.
Nada se quedó con nada:
todo volvió entre las olas.
Y aquel anhelo gracioso
que la llevó entre sonrisas
le pone sobre la cara
nuevo antifaz soñoliento.
El empañado recuerdo
se asoma por los cristales
como viajero que pide
la limosna de la noche.
Y los ojos lo recogen
en su espejito pequeño
y juegan a luz y sombra
de las manos a la playa.

AT the window again
alone with the horizon.
The afternoon comes and goes,
aeroplane of her dream.
Everything goes away into the distance.
Nothing remains at her side.
The sea makes spangles
for its yellow tambourine.
Nothing is forgotten:
not even the silk handkerchief.
Nothing is left of anything:
all is lost in the waves.
And that graceful desire
that carried her away smiling
puts a dreamy new veil
on her face.
Memory's shadow
appears at the window
like a traveler
begging alms from the night.
And her eyes gather the memory
in the tiny mirror
and with her hands
she plays light and shadow
on the beach.

Poemas de la Isla

The Island Poems

ALTAS ventanas abiertas
dejaron sombras de luces
disparadas en la arena.
El camino estaba quieto,
muerto del blanco preciso
con doce heridas de invierno.
En las ramas de los pinos
el pensamiento giraba
las brisas de los olivos.
Una vez cerca. El espacio
vacío, libre, perdido
a lo largo de los brazos.
Y qué lejos el momento,
cuatro paredes baratas
imágenes del espejo.
Ni tú ni yo. Las ventanas
altas, abiertas, desnudas,
suicidas de madrugada.

HIGH open windows
left shadows of scattered
lights on the sand.
The street was quiet,
dead from the white precision
of winter's twelve wounds.
In the pine's branches
thought swirls
breezes through the olives.
Once close. Empty
space, free, lost
along my arms.
And how distant the moment,
those four cheap walls—
images from a mirror.
Not you, not I. The high,
open, naked windows—
suicides of dawn.

Yo no sé por cuál vereda
he de encontrarme tu sombra
ni dónde hallaré la huella
de tu andar desconocido.
Y voy con los ojos bajos
contando las piedrecitas,
y sujetando en prisiones
de párpados y latidos
todos los grises contornos
que el sol dibuja en el suelo
y todas las curvas blancas
que el aire forma en la tierra.
Yo no sé por qué camino
ni cuál será la vereda.

ON which of these pathways
will I find your shadow?
Where will I find the track
of your unknown going?
I walk, eyes lowered,
counting the pebbles,
condemning to prisons
of eyelids and heartbeats
all of the grey outlines
which the sun draws in the dirt
and every white curve
that air forms on the earth.
I don't know which road
nor which path it will be.

ESTE juego conocido,
cuatro paredes a oscuras,
espacios desorientados,
inseguridad del aire
por distancias ignoradas,
proximidad inconcreta
—¿por dónde vino la noche?—
Y se confunde la imagen,
tacto, forma, complicado
adivinar de lo oculto.
Este juego conocido
sin el principio ni el fin,
mirada abierta en la sombra,
—y la luz ¿por dónde está?—

THIS well-known game,
four darkened walls,
confusing spaces,
the air's insecurity
through unknown distances,
vague proximity—
where does the night come from?
The image becomes confused,
touch, form, complicated
the divining of the occult.
This well-known game
without beginning or end,
an open look in the shadow,
and the light, where is it coming from?

QUE repetido deseo,
todo igual y siempre el mismo,
distinto y otro, inconsciente,
confundido y tan preciso,
se me va quedando dentro
escondido y dueño solo,
perdido y presente siempre.
Altas noches, muros largos,
patios de la madrugada.
Y mi deseo rodando,
—número de circo—libre.
Una y otra vez, alerta
dando la voz en mis sienes,
centinela de mi pecho,
fiel compañero constante.
Qué repetido deseo
tan inseguro y tan firme,
ignorada certidumbre.
Distancia, viento y espacio.

THAT recurring desire,
where everything's equal and always the same,
distinct and different, unconscious,
confused, yet so precise,
beginning to hide itself within me,
my lone master,
drifting yet always present.
Long nights and walls,
patios of dawn . . .
And my circling desire—
a circus act—free.
Time and time again, always ready
voice throbbing in my temples,
sentinel of my breast,
faithful constant companion.
Ever constant desire
so unsure, yet so reliable,
doubtful certainty.
Distance, wind and space . . .

QUE todas las noches fueran
así, dentro de mis ojos,
repetidos e incontables
sueños para la alegría.
Soñar, y luego despierta
libre y ligera en el aire,
claridades del recuerdo
interrogación segura.
Que yo pudiera pensar
—sueño, sombras, almohada,—
cada noche incomparable
mi bordada fantasía.
Frentecita de la aurora
sienes de la madrugada.
¡Qué sopor de bienvenida
en mi anhelo sobre el mar!

WERE that all my nights were thus—
in my eyes—
recurring, uncountable
dreams of happiness.
Dreaming, and later awake,
free and light in the air—
lucid memories,
ever present questions.
That I *could* think—
dream, shadows, pillow,—
each incomparable night
my embroidered fantasy.
Little forehead of the dawn,
temples of morning.
What deep sleep of welcome
in my longing for the sea!

MAR redondo, desvelado,
sortija blanca,
novio enamorado.
Desde el balcón,
por la orilla, rizando
va mi canción.
Mar de siete colores,
curva salada,
cinturón de novia enamorada.
En mi ventana
se ha prendido el encaje
de la mañana.
Mar abierto, encandilado,
verde collar,
novio enamorado.
Desde el balcón,
por la orilla, rodando
mi corazón.

CIRCULAR, unsleeping sea,
blond ringlet of hair,
young man in love.
My song goes rippling
along the shore
from my balcony.
Sea of seven colors,
salted curve,
sash of a young woman in love.
The lace of morning
hangs in my window.
Open, dazzling sea,
green necklace,
a young man in love.
From the balcony
my heart
wanders along the shore.

CAMINITO de la noche
dime dónde vas
con tus cuatro palabras
sin acabar.
Que por donde está el río
no viene la mar
y viene y va.
¡Ay, qué solo, sin luces
ni voces para madrugar!
Caminito de la noche
guárdamelo del mal.
Pero no te pierdas
torrecita de plata
luna de cristal.

NEVERENDING pathway of the night,
tell me in a few words
where you go.
It's not along this pathway,
though it comes and goes,
that the river runs to the sea.
How alone you must be without lights
or voices to wake up to!
Night's pathway,
protect me from evil.
Silver tower,
crystal moon,
don't stray from me!

CERCA. Palabra inútil.
Yo te busco
por donde llega mi distancia.
Cerca.
Seguro instante de sorpresas.
Dormido vuelo alzado
de mí, por mí.
Cerca.
Donde mi corazón te sienta:
pulso del mar,
tictac de la ausencia,
caminito seguro,
vaivén.
Cerca.
Donde la indecisión no deje
huella.
Donde palabra,
vuelta,
marque un signo seguro.
Cerca.

FENCE. Useless word.
I look for you
however far I go.
Fence.
Sure instant of surprise.
Sleepy thought sent into flight
from me, by me.
Fence.
Where my heart feels you:
pulse of the sea,
tick-tack of absence,
sure pathway,
going only to return.
Fence.
Where indecision leaves
no trace.
Where word,
returning,
leaves one sure sign.
Fence.

CRINES de la noche,
caballo perdido de la madrugada.
Cristales desnudos,
piel estremecida,
transparencia larga.
¡Qué escondido sueño por orillas blancas
y violento y mudo
galopar del alba!
Estanques dormidos,
caderas flexibles de la noche intacta.
Cansado desvelo
viento desvelado
humedad cansada.
¡Qué escondido sueño bajo orillas blancas
y qué lento, inmóvil
galopar del alba!

NIGHT'S mane,
lost horse of dawn.
Fine and lustrous hair,
of long transparencies,
shivering skin.
What hidden dream along the white shores
violent and silent
galloping of the dawn!
Sleeping pools of water,
flexible haunches of the whole night.
Weary vigilance —
unsleeping wind —
weary humidity . . .
What hidden dream under the white shores
and how solemn, the motionless
galloping of the dawn!

QUISIERA tener muy alto
una ventana pequeña.
Mar y cielo todo el día
que se me entraran por ella.
Prendida como un lucero
mi ventanita despierta.
De la mañana a la noche
cantando mi voz alerta.
Todo el sol y todo el aire
para adornarme la espera.
¡Ay, quién tuviera muy alto
ventana chica y abierta!

WOULD that I had one
small, high window.
So that all day the sea and the sky
would come through it to me.
My awakened window
flaming like a lantern.
My bright voice singing
from morning to night.
All of the sun and all the air
to adorn my waiting.
Who wouldn't want
a small, high, open window!

EL cielo limpio de nubes
recién lavadito está.
La luna, sola, en su fondo
abierta de par en par.
Peregrino por el cielo
caminar y caminar
y entrar en la luna blanca
y abierta de par en par.

THE recently scrubbed sky
is swept clean of clouds.
The moon, alone, in the background,
opens from time to time.
I make my way through the sky
walking and walking
and enter the white moon
which opens from time to time.

LA luz dejó caer
su moneda redonda
y sobre la moneda
de luz, quedó mi mano
abierta a la limosna.
Alrededor la sombra
acarició el contorno
de las cosas dormidas.
Yo me sentía feliz
perdida, sin reflejos,
en las paredes libres.
Sólo mi mano atenta
desdoblada segura
su única presencia.
El afilado borde
de luz sobre la sombra
sacrificó mi mano
en su bandeja intacta.
Una, dos, tres...inútil
péndulo de las horas.

LIGHT dropped its
round coin,
and over the coin
of light my hand
reached out,
open for alms.
The shadow embraced
the entire neighborhood
of sleeping things.
I was happily lost,
casting no reflections,
within free walls.
Only my waiting hand
firmly unfolded
its unique presence.
The sharp edge
of light over the shadow
sacrificed my hand
on its untouched platter.
One, two, three . . . useless
pendulum of hours.

Por el viento y por la brisa
la lluvia viene cantando
su canción de prometida.
Sacude todas las hojas
del olivo y de la encina
y multiplica sus notas
temblorosas de alegría.
La lluvia vino cantando
irisada de sonrisas
y dejó mi traje blanco
bordado de armonía.
Regalo de la mañana
sobre mi frente prendida
en un acorde brillante
y húmedo, de medio día.

THROUGH the wind and breeze
the rain comes singing
its song of the betrothed.
It shakes all the leaves
of the olives and oaks
and multiplies
their tremulous notes of joy.
The rain comes singing,
curled with smiles,
and leaves my dress white,
embroidered with harmony.
Gift of the morning
on my shining forehead
in a brilliant, humid
harmony of midday. . . .

UNA huella de luz sobre la tarde
alarga el horizonte y se confunde
en una telaraña de visiones.
Dueño de su distancia incomparable
tú llevas el vaivén sobre las curvas
como ágil marinero de tus años.
El sol busca reflejos a tu sombra
en cada vuelta azul de tu peligro.
Y la tarde se llena de milagros,
cristal abierto de los arco iris
como una estrella blanca perseguida.

ACROSS the afternoon, a trace of light
lengthens the horizon, and mixes
with a cobweb of visions.
Master of incomparable distance,
you bring it rocking over the waves
like the agile mariner of your years.
The sun searches for your shadow's reflections
in every blue turn of your danger.
And the afternoon is full of miracles,
the rainbow's open window,
like a pale star pursued.

About the Translator

The translator, Carlos Reyes, has published four books of poems, including *The Shingle Weaver's Journal,* a finalist for the Elliston Prize, *Nightmarks* and *A Suitcase Full of Crows,* a finalist for the 1996 Oregon Book Award. His poems, prose, and translations have been widely anthologized and have appeared in such journals as *Antioch Review, Willow Springs, and Black Warrior Review.* He lives in Portland, Oregon, with his partner Elizabeth Atly, a designer and videographer, and travels to Ireland, where he maintains a seventeenth century cottage.